100% unofficial

Animal Crossing New Horizons

Residents' Handbook

KINGFISHER
LONDON & NEW YORK

Copyright © Macmillan Publishers International Ltd 2020
Published in the United States by Kingfisher
120 Broadway, New York, NY 10271
Kingfisher is a division of Macmillan Children's Books, London
All rights reserved.

Distributed in the U.S. and Canada by Macmillan,
120 Broadway, New York, NY 10271

Library of Congress Cataloging-in-Publication data has been applied for.

ISBN: 978-0-7534-7798-4

Written by Claire Lister
Designed, edited and project managed by Dynamo Limited

Kingfisher books are available for special promotions and premiums. For details contact:
Special Markets Department, Macmillan, 120 Broadway, New York, NY 10271.

For more information, please visit
www.kingfisherbooks.com

9 8 7 6 5 4 3 2 1
1TR/1220/WKT/RV/128MA

100% unofficial

Animal Crossing New Horizons

Residents' Handbook

KINGFISHER
LONDON & NEW YORK

Welcome!

Whether you have no idea who Tom Nook is or you're a longstanding Animal Crossing fan, this is the book for you. Find out about the tiny details that make New Horizons so special, and learn how to make the most **Bells** in the shortest time, so you can maximize your deserted island experience.

The book is divided into three sections:

• **Island Basics**—this part is ideal for people just starting the game, but it is also full of tips and facts for all players.
• **Island Life**—this section will help you make the most of the game.
• **Island Designer**—take true control of your island and how it looks!

Contents

Getting Started

You've heard the buzz (hopefully not a wasps' nest ... more about that later!), now it's time to start your New Horizons island life.

If you haven't already started the game, don't worry about preparing yourself beforehand—it's best to just jump straight in and book your very own **Nook Inc. Deserted Island Getaway Package**. Two of your new animal friends, Timmy and Tommy, will help you through the process. Pick your character name, and add your birthday (prepare yourself for some awesome Animal Crossing fun when your special day comes around). Next up—create your avatar. Don't worry too much at this point—you can change whatever you like later, from hairstyle to skin tone and gender.

You'll get loads more hair color and style options later.

Confirm

Staying Safe Online

The great thing about Animal Crossing is that you can have plenty of fun playing offline. In fact, there's no need to go online at all. If your parent or carer decides it's OK to visit other islands or have other players visit your island, here are a few essentials ...

• Only ever open your island up to people you know IRL (in real life).
• If anyone ever sends a message that makes you feel uncomfortable, tell a grown-up and report the message to Nintendo.
• Never share any personal information online. Turn to pages 44–45 to find out more about what friends can and can't do on each others' islands.

Timmy

There is so much to look forward to! But first, let us introduce ourselves. I'm Timmy with Nook Inc.

Location Is Key

Now you will need to opt for either the northern or southern hemisphere. Timmy and Tommy recommend choosing the same hemisphere that you live in IRL—that way, after your first night on the island, if it's summer outside, it's summer in the game, and when it's nighttime outside, it's dark in the game.

During the first evening, you will be able to pick a name for your island. Choose wisely—you can't change it later!

Did you spot this hidden beach? When you meet Redd, this location becomes super important.

Lighter-colored green patches show the higher ground.

Choose Your Island!

Dark-green grass and yellow sand are all at sea level.

You won't be able to cross rivers at first.

The Nook Inc. logo will show you where **Resident Services** will be located.

Here's the airport. This is where you will arrive, and where you can book trips to other islands.

Island Selection

Now we get to the important part—picking your island. You will be shown four islands, all with roughly the same land mass, so don't worry too much about this decision, just go with the layout that looks good to you.

It's In-Tents!

After your seaplane drops off you and the first two animal islanders, it's time to meet Tom Nook, the raccoon in charge of the Deserted Island Getaway Package. He'll instruct you to pick up a tent from Timmy or Tommy, and then figure out where to pitch it. It's worth spending a little time finding the perfect spot—if you're too close to a river, you might not be able to get around it easily. Eventually, you will be able to move it, but not for a while.

Island Basics

I set up my tent! That's a big first step!

Camera

Nook Miles

Critterpedia

Custom Designs

Best Friends list

Rescue Service

Chat Log

Nook Miles +

Nook Miles +

Island Designer

DIY Recipes

Map that shows you where all the buildings are

Passport

Call Islander

At Your Fingertips

After your first night on the island, Tom Nook will present you with your very own **NookPhone**. This is your go-to gadget for island life, but not all of the functions will be available immediately.

Key Players

At first, there are a handful of animals on your island. Time to get to know them and why they're important ...

In Animal Crossing, Tom Nook is the person who you owe it all to. And by that, we mean that you literally are in debt to him! Luckily, it's much easier to earn money in Animal Crossing than it is in real life, so don't worry TOO much about the bill he presents you with on your first morning. He claims it's modest, but even though the amount sounds far from it (just wait until later in the game!), don't let it get you down.

Tom is your main guide to the island, along with his nephews Timmy and Tommy. At first, they can be found at the **Resident Services** tent. Tom Nook will set you tasks to help you get going, and Timmy will let you sell him almost anything you can find on the island. He also has a number of items for sale each day. Finally, Tommy will be wandering around the island—flag him down if you need any help.

After learning how to use a DIY workbench, you can make tools, furniture, and all kinds of other goodies.

Craftable

The island representative badge shows on the passport.

Resident Rep.

PASSPORT

Add a short comment to your profile.

🦀 Coral Coast   🍒 Cherries

Very First Island Dweller

Blossom

Island Basics

You can unlock other words to use in your title by earning **Nook Miles**.

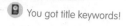

You got title keywords!

Legendary   Walking Dictionary

You got Nook Miles!

3,000

Island Representative

If you're the lead player on your island, it means that there are certain things that only you can do. Tom Nook will give you tasks to undertake. You won't always know why, but it's always worth doing what he asks since it unlocks new parts of the game. Early on, Tom Nook will ask to see anything you catch with your shiny, new fishing rod—make sure that you bring him some fish as quickly as you can.

Watch what your animal friends do—some might exercise, sing, or just chill out!

When one of the animals really likes you, they will give you a nickname.

First Two Islanders

There are more than 390 different animals that might come to live on your island. The first two that move to the island are randomly generated at the start of the game. Chat to your new buddies as often as you can to discover their personalities and what they like. Try giving them presents, and see how they react.

9

Island Economy

Take the time to learn how money works on your island, and you will soon get ahead. You can bank on it!

You might find the first morning on your island something of a rude awakening when you're presented with an itemized bill for **49,800 Bells**! Shock will probably turn into confusion when you're told that you can pay off the debt in a completely different currency, and you now owe Tom Nook 5,000 **Nook Miles**. Take a deep breath, and we'll clear things up. **Bells** are the main currency, and you can earn them by selling items to Timmy and Tommy (and some other fun ways you'll discover later). **Nook Miles** are another form of currency that you earn by living your best island life—so just relax and you'll pay this debt off in no time. Oh, and we hate to break it to you, but this first debt will pale into insignificance as you progress through the game.

How much would you like to pay?

| Loan Balance | 548, 000 | Bells |
| Savings Balance | 562, 312 | Bells |

548, 000
Bells

C	Full Amount	
7	8	9
4	5	6
1	2	3

Confirm

You can deposit or withdraw money at the **ABD (Automatic Bell Dispenser)** in **Resident Services**.

It is better to save up your **Bells** until you can pay off your debt in one big chunk. That way, you will earn interest on your savings at the beginning of each month.

Island Basics

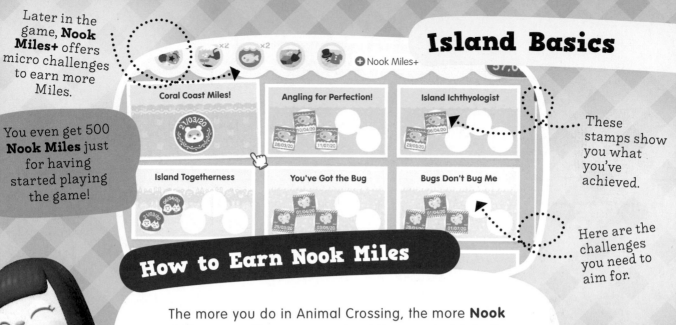

Coral Coast Miles!

Angling for Perfection!

Island Ichthyologist

Island Togetherness

You've Got the Bug

Bugs Don't Bug Me

Later in the game, **Nook Miles+** offers micro challenges to earn more Miles.

You even get 500 **Nook Miles** just for having started playing the game!

These stamps show you what you've achieved.

Here are the challenges you need to aim for.

How to Earn Nook Miles

The more you do in Animal Crossing, the more **Nook Miles** you will earn. So, get out there and pick fruit, catch fish and bugs, bash rocks, take photos, talk to your fellow islanders … and so much more. When you hit certain milestones, you will be awarded **Nook Miles**. Keep track of your progress by checking your **NookPhone**—this is especially useful when chasing that first 5,000 **Nook Miles**.

Coconuts

How to Earn Bells

Don't get too used to paying your debt in **Nook Miles**—this is a one-time-only opportunity, and all future debt is in **Bells**. But by the time you're switching currency, you will probably have a feel for the best ways to earn **Bells**. Timmy will buy any resources you don't need, and until you upgrade your tent to a house, you will be oh-so glad since you will soon run out of pocket space!

Running out of room? Your pockets can fill up quickly even after upgrading them.

Tool Up!

There are a few key items you will need to make or buy to live life to the fullest in Animal Crossing ...

One of the first things you'll learn to do in New Horizons is make a flimsy fishing rod, but this is just the start. To progress through the game, you will need recipes for tools that will help you do new things. Also, tools break, as you might have guessed from the fact that so many of the basic ones are called flimsy—so be prepared to make some of them again and again ... and again. Look for better tools that don't break as often. You can either buy upgraded recipes from the **Nook Stop** or more durable equipment from **Nook's Cranny**. But even these improved versions don't last forever.

Click on a gray shovel to add a shortcut to one of the tools in your pockets.

Use the left stick to highlight the tool you want, and press A to hold it.

Tool Ring

One of the most useful things to spend your **Nook Miles** on is the super-helpful **Tool Ring**. It only costs 800 **Nook Miles**, but will save you loads of time when switching between tools. When you've bought it, press up on the D-pad of your left Joy-Con, and the ring appears—you can now quickly select the right tool for the job.

Fishing Rod

Patience is key if you want to land a whopper!

Net

Don't let the insects bug you out—catch them with a net.

Axe

You might find it useful to carry both an axe and a stone axe—use the stone version to get wood from trees without chopping them down.

Vaulting Pole

Crossing a river has never been easier with this unbreakable tool.

Shovel

Dig up manila clams along the beach to make bait for fishing.

Watering Can

Look for cute watering cans like this one, which is shaped like an elephant.

Ladder

You'll need this to get to higher ground before you can build inclines. This tool NEVER breaks!

Slingshot

Shoot down all kinds of surprises with this—just make sure you are right under the balloon carrying the present across the skies.

Umbrella

You never know when you'll be caught in a rainstorm!

When you hit certain targets, you will be rewarded with golden versions of some of the tools!

Wand

Change your outfit with a wave of a wand.

Fan

Keep your cool in a heatwave with this.

Be Resourceful

Your island paradise is full of natural resources that you can tap into to use for crafting or decoration.

To make it anywhere in this game, you'll need to gather resources—they will be the building blocks of your island. Whether you need to make yourself a tool, boost your **Bells,** or help out the cultural endeavours of the island, everything you could want is there—you just need to know where to find it. Many players find it useful to set up a daily routine for how they work their way around the island, making the most of what's available.

Make time each day to ...

- ☑ Run a complete circuit of the island to collect seashells and catch fish.

- ☑ Go for a swim—dive for other sea creatures and pearls.

- ☑ Explore the interior of the island with a net in hand to catch bugs.

- ☑ Shake trees to collect branches and fruit, or even **Bells** and furniture!

- ☑ Use a flimsy or stone axe on trees to harvest wood, so that you don't chop them down.

- ☑ Use an axe or shovel on rocks to harvest stone, iron, gold, clay, and sometimes even **Bells**.

- ☑ Dig any glowing holes for buried **Bells** or cracked earth for fossils.

Island Basics

Eating fruit fills you with super strength, so you can dig up a tree or break a big rock.

Trees Are Good

One of the first things to try is shaking a tree to see what falls out. Hardwood trees tend to drop up to five branches at a time, and fruit trees also drop fruit (obviously!). What you might not expect, however, is that someone has been hiding furniture up trees, so it's always worth giving them a quick shake, just in case. But watch out! If you disturb a wasp's nest, be prepared to get stung—unless you're quick enough to get your net out and catch the swarm!

Fruit can even be used to make furniture!

Always keep a stash of medicine to treat stings, or simply wear a stylish pair of shades to cover up your swollen eye!

What to Keep and What to Sell

To start with, you will probably want to sell most things simply to make more **Bells**, but some things are definitely worth keeping. It's wise to keep a stash of the different kinds of wood, some iron, and some clay, as these are the basis of many DIY recipes. Crafted items sell for more than the raw materials they're made from, so that's good to know. You might also be tempted to pick and sell all the weeds on your island, but try not to sell them all because you'll never know what recipes you might need them for.

Fins, Wings, 'n' Things

Get to know the wildlife of your island, and you'll find a whole new appreciation for nature ... and how you can benefit from it!

Not all of the resources on the island are as easy to get hold of as rocks or branches. Arm yourself with a net, a rod, and a shovel to really reap the riches that the island has on offer! Your island is teeming with life and buried marvels. Fossils and buried treasure are easiest to find—just look for cracked earth or a glowing spot, and dig. Dig sites are updated each day and the locations vary, so if you can't find any one morning, check behind a few trees. Take any fossils you find to Blathers (see page 24) to identify.

If you dig up **Bells**, plant them back in the glowing hole to grow a money tree and triple your cash!

Fossils are a great way to fill the museum or sell for **Bells**.

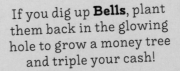

Island Basics

Tarantulas and scorpions can make you LOADS of money, especially if you land on a mystery island filled with them (see page 42).

A Bug's Life

All you need to catch the various bugs that you share the island with is a net and patience. Common butterflies aren't too fast and are easy to catch, but some bugs are jumpy—and we're not just talking grasshoppers—so you need to creep up on them. When you have your net out, hold A to slowly tiptoe your way closer, then release the button to swipe down with your net.

Make sure you read the puns whenever you catch something new.

I caught an earth-boring dung beetle! It's not boring at all!

The One That Got Away

At first, fishing is a little bit trickier than catching bugs, but all you need to do is perfect your technique. Aim just in front of the fish—sometimes to one side and diagonally in front works—wait until the float bobs under the water and you hear a "dddkkk" sound as the fish nibbles—then press A. Your controller will vibrate as your character reels in the fish—the greater the vibrations, the bigger the fish!

You can even catch fish that are bigger than your character!

17

Getting Crafty

It's time to get down to work. To make the most of your island life, you will need to collect resources and recipes ...

You've probably been handed a recipe card, but you may not know what to do with it. Now it's time to take Tom Nook up on his offer of a DIY workshop. Get yourself down to **Resident Services** to open up a huge part of the game! After Tom Nook teaches you how to make a fishing rod out of five tree branches, you can read any DIY recipe to learn it. You'll want to build a workbench as your own dedicated crafting spot. You can even carry it around with you to craft on the go!

If you need to sell things when the store is closed, you drop them here, but be warned: if you sell items this way, you'll get 20% fewer bells than you do selling inside the shop.

Press A while looking at the message board to find out the **Hot Items** of the day.

Furniture and More

Crafting isn't just about tools—it's a great way to make furniture for your house. Or you could make a stack of **Bells** by making and selling **Hot Items** to Timmy and Tommy—each day there are up to two craftable items that they will buy for double the normal number of **Bells**. Just ask them, or check the message board outside **Nook's Cranny** to find out what to craft each day.

Here are the top five ways
to gather new recipes:

☑ Look for bottles washed up
on the beach—they always
contain a recipe.

☑ Some balloons carry DIY
recipes—use a slingshot
to bring them down.

☑ Visit your fellow islanders—if
they are crafting something,
they will often share the
recipe with you.

☑ When you find certain items,
you can be inspired to come
up with your own DIY recipes.

☑ For some recipes that
are truly out of this world,
chat to Celeste when
she's visiting.

Make sure you buy the **Pretty Good Tools** recipes from the **Nook Stop** in **Resident Services**, so that you can craft stronger tools that don't break as often.

Tap A repeatedly while crafting to speed up the action.

If you get hold of the right recipe, you could build a more sophisticated **Workbench** like this.

OK, that's all the basic stuff, so let's go and live the island life!

Your House

What will you probably spend the most time and money on in Animal Crossing New Horizons? That's right! Your house.

Although there's a whole island to explore, there's no place like home. From the very beginning of the game, you are saving **Nook Miles** to upgrade your tent into a house, but it doesn't stop there. Oh, no! Soon, you'll be trying to earn as many **Bells** as possible to increase the size of your house by adding room after room.

Of course, each extra room will cost you more and more. Apart from giving you another area to theme and furnish, the house upgrades also increase your storage space—essential for any islander who likes to hoard resources, furniture, clothes, or just about anything else!

Looks like it's time to add another room!

Room Types

At first, you will only have one room and will probably fill it very quickly with all kinds of furniture. When you only have a couple of rooms, they will each have to serve multiple purposes, so try and create zones with different uses. You can use a folding screen to divide a room into living and sleeping spaces. But make sure you don't put things in the same room that don't belong together— who wants a toilet in their kitchen?!

Be warned! Cockroaches will appear in your house if you haven't played the game for a long time!

Island Life

It's tempting to put all of the furniture around the edge of a room, but it doesn't always look good. Try to make sure there's a central focus, such as a rug or a table.

Natural

Use the patterns that Mabel gives you to give your furniture a theme.

Happy Home

Pay off your house debt, and you can add another room!

Every house in Animal Crossing receives a **Happy Home Academy (HHA)** evaluation. Essentially, this means that your house is rated on a number of different criteria and awarded points. When you reach a certain number of points, you will get awards that you can display in your house (you could even have a whole wall dedicated to your achievements). To boost your rating, try and use furniture that's all the same color or part of a specially themed set.

Interior Decorator

Now that you know the basics, it's time to have fun with your house ...

It's tempting to decorate each room with a proper function like you have in your real home. You will find plenty of things to fill a kitchen/diner, and you can have a cute bedroom, with posters on the wall, a bed, wardrobe, bookshelf, and even a pet hamster. Use plants and small items, and hang pictures on the walls to add detail that really make the place feel like home. It might be more fun, however, to create a space that's completely different. You can take a look in the houses of some of the animals you share your island with for some inspiration.

A few simple adjustments can make a HUGE difference to a room.

Room Planner

It can be tricky to get furniture and accessories just where you want them, so you'll want to click the down button on the D-pad on the left-hand controller to enter a mode that makes arranging your room MUCH easier. You can rotate items and move them around to get the perfect positioning.

Tex's house is dedicated to his music. It's so cool, it's ice cold!

The animals on your island love to coordinate their furniture.

Julian's house is as magical as you would expect a unicorn's to be!

If you can grow enough bamboo, you could have a zen room like this.

Some animals enjoy the finer things, and this is reflected in their room!

Daisy has a room as cute as she is. Visit her at home for DIY recipes.

Zucker loves snacks, and his house feels like a street food market.

Like Mallary, you can bring the outside inside your house!

Or you could go for a random room, lined with logs and filled with cake!

Curly is very house-proud, so you might find him dusting.

Some animals have a color theme, like this mellow yellow room.

Your house is a work in progress—it takes awhile to get what you want.

Blathers and His Museum

When your first visitor, an owl named Blathers, moves in, it's time to bring your island's culture to life!

Soon after settling on your island, Tom Nook will ask for donations of bugs and fish for a mysterious friend of his. Gather up five different specimens, and give them to Tom as soon as you can. The next day, Blathers will move into a new tent on your island. Soon, you will love this odd owl, who is obsessed with fossils (he'll give you a shovel recipe so you can finally start digging some up), and repulsed by insects. Blathers will only take one sample of each fossil, fish, or insect, so check your **NookPhone**—any insect or fish he already has will have a little owl beside it. After just 15 more donations, the tent will be upgraded to a real museum! Now you have the huge job of filling it on your hands ...

Like most owls, Blathers sleeps during the day, so you'll have to wake him up!

All dreams start small! Blathers' dream begins in this humble field tent.

When your museum opens, make sure you go to the celebration.

24

Island Life

Queen Alexandra's birdwing

If there's an owl like this beside an insect in your **Critterpedia**, it means Blathers already has one at the museum.

Insect Wing

If you turn left when you enter the museum, you'll find yourself in a tropical greenhouse filled with all the bugs and insects that Blathers so despises. Head to the far left to get to the butterfly house, and watch all the beautiful creatures fly around.

Every so often, you might manage to land a whopper like this oarfish ...

Blathers

Hoo! Dare I say, EWW! That is a mantis!

Blathers REALLY doesn't like insects!

Aquarium Wing

... give it to Blathers, so you can see it in its full glory whenever you like.

Turn right after entering the museum to step into an underwater delight! The fish and underwater creatures are grouped in tanks according to their natural habitat. A stroll through your Animal Crossing aquarium is a wonderfully calming way to spend some time.

Behind the Scenes at the Museum

Your museum is more than an aquarium and a butterfly house. Why not explore the dinosaur rooms?

All of the fossils you dig up look the same—a white ammonite on a blue slab—but when you take them to Blathers, he will identify exactly what they are. Some of your finds are small and self-contained, like coprolite (fossilized dino poop!), but one of the most satisfying elements of building up the museum's collection in New Horizons is gradually building up the huge dinosaur skeletons part by part.

You might be wondering what the colored lines snaking through the fossil section mean. If you follow one of them all the way to the final room, you will find a row of animal silhouettes—the lines show how each creature evolved. Try standing in the position on the far right, and see what happens.

The star shape probably means a fossil can be found.

Trace the evolution of different animals, including humans.

Piece by piece, huge dinosaur remains will build up.

Sadly, Blathers will only accept one of each type of fossil. At the beginning of the game, he will take most of them, but as you progress, you will need to decide what to do with the surplus …

Sell them! You can sell fossils for a tidy sum at **Nook's Cranny**.

Start your own fossil museum in your house or maybe a remote part of your island.

Trade them with your friends on other islands. This will help each of you to complete your museum's collection.

You can get up to **6,000 Bells** for each dino part you sell!

You could dedicate a whole room in your house to dinosaurs—or create an outdoor museum of your own.

Game Idea

Invite friends to your island, and you could have a game of hide-and-seek in the museum. Choose who will do the seeking, and ask them to close their eyes IRL for 10 seconds. This should give everyone else enough time to run away into their chosen area and hide. If the seeker has a timer (you can buy them in **Nook's Cranny**), set it for three minutes, and see how many friends they can find in that time.

Remember that you need to hold B down if you want your character to run.

02:06 00 00 00

27

An Artistic Eye?

So, bugs, fish, and dinosaurs aren't enough for you? Sounds like you'll enjoy the art gallery.

Watch for a fox named Redd visiting your island. He is very entertaining—just don't believe all he says. Redd is an art dealer, but not everything he has for sale is the genuine article. You'll probably get suspicious (and rightly so) when he claims you're his cousin and offers you a family discount—he does this to

EVERYONE! After your first encounter, Redd will turn up from time to time on **Jolly Redd's Treasure Trawler**, which drops anchor on your secret beach on the north of the island (you'll probably have to use a ladder to get to it). Each time he arrives, he will have four pieces of art from around the world for you to choose from—you are only allowed to buy one item per day. Sometimes they will all be real, sometimes they will all be fake, and sometimes it will be a mix. It's impossible to predict!

Keep your eyes peeled for **Redd's Treasure Trawler** and step inside ...

... to buy some art. But watch out, he might be scamming you!

What's going on with the eyebrows on the *Mona Lisa*?!

The genuine article will be added to the museum's collection.

How to Spot a Forgery

It can be really tricky to figure out when Redd is trying to pull a fast one. If you've ever seen a picture of the real piece of art IRL, you might be able to spot if something is wrong, but it's not always easy.

Things to watch for:
- Coffee stains on the art
- Strange eyebrows
- Parts of the painting missing
- Statues with something strange added

Blathers

HOO-WHAT?!

Art Collector

When you take your newly purchased art to Blathers, if he declares it to be fake, don't worry too much. After all, you still have something that ALMOST looks like a priceless masterpiece. You could dedicate one room in your house to art and have your very own gallery of fakery. Or you could use the sculpture forgeries to decorate your island and have a sculpture park.

Shops and Salescreatures

Timmy and Tommy are there from the get-go, but they're not the only shopkeepers on the island ...

The museum isn't the only building on your island—there are stores and stands too! **Nook's Cranny** will remain your go-to shop in New Horizons, with its daily rotation of special items, wallpaper, and flooring. But in time, a clothes store will be added into the mix, as well as a host of traveling salescreatures who drop by.

Able Fashion

Mabel Able is one such traveling salescreature, who, along with her sister, Sable, sets up a permanent store—cannily called **Able Sisters**—that really opens up the fashion possibilities. The central display changes daily, and the mannequins on the left change weekly, while the back wall displays custom designs created by players. Pop into the changing room and try on whatever combo takes your fancy.

Mabel is always happy to help you in your adventures in fashion.

Browse the store, then try on outfits in the changing room.

Can You Kick It?

Sometimes Kicks, the shoe-selling skunk, will appear outside **Resident Services** selling socks, shoes, and bags. Buying items from him is a good way to up your accessories game.

Out-of-This-World Rugs!

From time to time, you may stumble upon Saharah, a camel who wanders around selling rugs, flooring, and wallpaper. The catch is—you don't know what you'll get until after you've handed over your hard-earned **Bells**. Every time you buy a rug from her, she will give you some **Saharah Tickets**. When you have five of them, you can swap them for a mysterious item. It's really worth investing in what she's selling, since you will be able to get hold of some amazingly different wallpaper and flooring—some of it is even animated!

The Third Able Sister

From time to time, Label (Mabel and Sable's sister) will visit your island. It's a good idea to talk to her, as it's an easy way of increasing your wardrobe without spending a single **Bell**. Label will ask for your help researching fashion designs by creating an outfit on a set theme. She will give you one piece of clothing, but you will need to find other elements to complete your look. She will reward you with a piece of clothing from her exclusive **Labelle** clothing line. She'll also send you **Tailor Tickets**, which you can use to buy any item up to the value of **3,000 Bells** at **Able Sisters**.

Some of Label's fashion research is a little out there!

Green Fingers

If you're aiming for five-star island status or a different way to earn Bells, planting flowers could be the answer.

Although you can buy some plants from **Nook's Cranny**, Lief the sloth brings a much wider variety, and you can buy shrubs from him, too. Flowers can be picked and sold, but shrubs will only flower at particular times of year.

With some careful planning, you can make sure your island always has a touch of color. While you can't make money out of shrubs, they do offer the option of a small hedge instead of fencing.

White-cosmos bag

Look at the plants for sale in the cabinet in **Nook's Cranny**.

Creating Color

Planting gardens for you and your fellow islanders is a cute way of making your island look better, but did you know that planting certain colors together can mean that hybrids grow? Flower varieties in Animal Crossing tend to come in three basic color options. Make sure you plant all of them together—you might get lucky and end up with pink lilies or even black roses!

You can sell hybrid flowers for more **Bells** than the regular colors.

Weeds: Good Or Bad?

You're encouraged to pick weeds at the beginning of the game and sell them. It can be a good way to earn **Nook Miles** or **Bells**, but weeds are also a fantastic resource for crafting—especially if you need medicine after getting stung by wasps—so don't ever run out. And even though you need to remove them to increase your island's star rating, they also have pretty flowers—after all, weeds are just plants growing where you don't want them.

Check out Lief's stock, and find a great selection of shrubs and seeds.

Use weeds to make DIY recipes like this one.

Weeds can look pretty, but they're useful, too.

Village People

New Horizons wouldn't be Animal Crossing without, guess what ... You got it! Animals.

Salescreatures aren't the only animals on your island. You can have a maximum of ten animals (as well as four human players) living on your island. You start off with the two who arrive with you, but how do others join you? You could leave it to chance and see who turns up, or you could get out there and meet some creatures. If you buy a ticket to a Mystery Island, you will sometimes find a random villager who you can talk to. If you like the animal, you can encourage them to move to your island. After you've built a campsite, you can chat to visiting animals, and they might want to move to your island permanently. But be careful: If your island is fully occupied, one of your current villagers could leave to make space for the newcomer—but you won't get a choice about who goes, so you could lose your favorite!

Curly

I just got here today, and I gotta say, this island's really nice! Feels perfect for step aerobics, nyoink.

Chat to campsite visitors, and they might move to your island.

If you see two villagers chatting, join in—you'll learn something about each of them, and it can be really funny.

Megan

This must be a great place to live if everyone's as friendly as you!

Island Life

Joy

Quests given to you by villagers are always worth completing as you will get a reward.

BFFs

Once you have various animals living on your island, you can interact with them in a number of different ways. Try and talk to them every day, give them presents (wrapped, if possible), and craft medicine if they're sick. They will also give you presents and teach you reactions, which are a great way of quickly communicating how you're feeling. There are many other interactions that you will find as you play. When your friendship reaches a certain level, a villager will present you with a framed photograph.

Frenemies

Just like in real life, you won't want to be best friends with every other animal. Some villagers have rather odd personalities, which is great if they're funny, but you might not like them or just want to spend a little time with others. Every so often, villagers will talk to you about the fact that they're thinking about moving away. If you encourage them to explore the world and leave, they will pack up and go, leaving space for a new villager to arrive. But if one of your BFFs asks about this, make sure you tell them to stay!

Zucker
Hey, Sparkle!
Sorry everything is so messy!
I'm packing up to move!

Animals Say the Funniest Things

With hundreds of possible villagers and conversation options, you'll never get bored on your island.

The villagers on your island all have their own obsessions and things they love talking about. From music and fashion, to kung fu movies and exercise, they will always have something to say. You will soon discover the animals you enjoy chatting to the most. Here are some of the funniest moments.

Mallary

Mallary

Well, hello. I take it you're finished giving me the silent treatment?

If you don't speak to a villager for awhile, be prepared for them to get rude or feel hurt.

Mallary

You know, it's OK to drop by and say hi without any particular reason. I'm always happy to chat with you.

The animals living on your island will talk to you about each other ... and sometimes you might need to help patch up their friendships.

Apple

A skirt! Of course! If you're going to be a pop star like me, you just have to have a fave fab skirt!

Villagers might react to something you're wearing or something close to where you're standing.

Island Life

Hippeux

Hippeux
I am a dancer, and this is my canvas! What do you mean, "Dancers don't use canvas"? I'm a dancer-painter!

Hippeaux likes to think he's sophisticated ...

Wilbur

Wilbur
Touchdown is like surfing the web in a toothbrush—we are parked and proud!

Your favorite pilot, Wilbur, always comes up with a weird and wonderful catchphrase.

Julian

Julian
Buongiorno, Blossom! I've been brushing up on my Spanish since we last met up.

Shhh! Nobody tell Julian that "buongiorno" is an Italian phrase, not Spanish!

Poncho

Poncho
Huh? You already knew? Wow, that rumor moved faster than my last marathon time, li'l bear.

Some villagers, such as Poncho, are obsessed with exercise.

Apple

Apple
Hi. I lost my voice. I was trying to be a heavy metal singer, instead of a pop star ... I am SO not metal.

This little hamster is one of our faves.

Pascal

Pascal
All things in moderation, including moderation. That's my recipe for chocolate-chip cookies, maaan.

Pascal has lots of deep and meaningful thoughts.

Your Island Year

Just like real life, things don't stay the same in Animal Crossing New Horizons. Make sure you're prepared and have the right clothes in your wardrobe for every season.

If you've done as the game suggests and opted for an island in the same hemisphere in which you live IRL, the seasons in the game should be identical to the seasons outside, but that's not the only variable. The weather on your island will change (but not necessarily mirror what you see outside your window), and this will affect the resources available, too. Certain bugs will only come out on hot days, while others thrive in the damp, and fishing after dark can result in a different catch. Dress yourself in cute T-shirts and shorts in the summer, but always have a raincoat or umbrella handy in case of rain.

There are loads of umbrella designs to collect.

Add Seasoning

In the real world, bugs and fish aren't necessarily found in the same place all year round, and it's just the same in Animal Crossing. Make sure you head out on the first day of each month to catch newcomers to donate to the museum, and tick them off in your **Critterpedia**. There are also various festivals and celebrations to look forward to throughout the year. Soon after the game launched, **Bunny Day** took place (it's the Animal Crossing version of Easter), with loads of eggs to collect and egg-themed DIY recipes to make. Keep an eye out for more celebrations throughout the year.

June is wedding season, with wedding-themed photo shoots on Harvey's island.

Every Sunday night during August, there is an amazing firework display and raffle.

Happy Birthday!

Make sure you play Animal Crossing on your real birthday. All of the villagers plan a special party for you, with presents, cake, and even a piñata! And make sure that you don't forget to give cupcakes to anyone who isn't at the party—they will each give you a present, too.

Everyone

HAPPY BIRTHDAAAAAY!

Swimming and Diving

Life on your island isn't limited to dry land alone. Grab yourself a wetsuit and snorkel, and explore the seas, too!

If your island is feeling a little busy, it might be worth taking some time out for a soothing swim in the sea. You don't need much equipment—just a snorkel and wetsuit, both of which can be bought from **Nook's Cranny** or **Nook Shopping**. When you've changed into the right apparel, simply run toward the sea and jump in by pressing A!

Game Idea

Get a group of friends together on your island for an underwater scavenger hunt. Set your friends a challenge, and see who wins ...

 First person to catch five different creatures.

 First person to catch three of the same creature.

Person who catches the most creatures in two minutes (use a timer for this one).

Make sure you have emptied your pockets as much as possible before diving, so you can gather as much as possible before coming back to dry land.

Island Life

**I got a scallop!
It otter be savoured.**

A Catchy Method

Diving might take a little practice, but it's worth it. As you're swimming around, press Y if you spot any bubbles. You will dive down, but the creature creating the bubbles will probably have moved a tad, so press A and swim in the direction of the bubbles. If you swim over the bubbles, you will collect the creature. You can't stay under the water for long, though, so you might need to dive down a few times.

**I got a gigas giant clam!
It's kind of a big deal.**

Sea Crafting

Pascal

Hey, maaan, about that scallop of yours ... Can I have it?

If you dive down and pick up a scallop, sometimes a sea otter named Pascal will bob around in the sea near you and ask for it. Be sure to give him the scallop—this little dude will always offer something in exchange. Sometimes it will be a pearl or a mermaid-inspired item of clothing, but it could also be a recipe for a mermaid set piece of furniture. Collect enough of them, and you could transform one of your rooms into an underwater wonderland!

Don't worry about swimming too far from shore—there's a net that keeps you from getting swept away!

41

Island Hopping

Want a change of scenery? No problem! There are countless islands to visit in Animal Crossing ...

Even the happiest villager in New Horizons gets wanderlust from time to time, and there's no reason why you wouldn't, too. Luckily, visiting other islands is a huge part of Animal Crossing, and the best thing is that you don't even need to go online to do it if you don't want to. You could visit islands to make new friends, collect resources, take photos, or even go on a challenge—on May 1st, in 2020, Tom Nook had a maze built that you could visit one time only for special rewards!

🎟 Bell voucher		
👉🎟 Nook Miles Ticket	📷	2
📱 Customizable phone case kit	📷	1
🌀 Sand path permit	📷	2,
🌀 Terra-cotta tile permit	📷	2,
Iron-and-stone fence	📷	1
Spiky fence	📷	1
Wave breaker	📷	1
Simple well	📷	

Have you noticed that the names of the **Dodo Airlines** staff are Wilbur and Orville? Just like the Wright brothers who invented the first powered airplane!

Orville

Hey, hey, hey! Welcome to your one and only gateway to the skies, The Coral Coast Airport.

It's a Mystery!

There are several kinds of deserted islands you can visit with a **Nook Miles Ticket**. You don't get to choose where you go, and you'll never visit the same island twice. So, why bother? You might meet an animal who could move to your island, but that's not the only reason—there are many different kinds of islands out there. If you stumble on one that has fruit trees you don't have on your own island, gather the fruit to sell or plant when you get back home (or you could just dig up the trees). Nonnative fruit always sells for more **Bells** than the fruit from trees when you start playing, so it's always worth planting other kinds of tree back home.

> 3 /10 Tarantula

If you're super lucky, you will find a tarantula or scorpion island. It will take time and patience, but if you fill your pockets with these bugs, you will be able to sell them for hundreds of thousands of **Bells**!

Visit Harvey

After you've progressed a certain way through the game, a dog named Harvey will visit your island and invite you to visit his. When you go to see him, you will find that he runs a photo studio, where you can use your villagers as models.

Harvey

After you introduced us, I thought I'd take a nice portrait and turn it into a poster. Hope you like it!

Visiting Friends' Islands

You can have lots of fun traveling to other islands and playing with friends online, but there are some crucial things to bear in mind.

There are two ways that other players can visit your island (or you can visit theirs). You can either open your gate to friends (this links to your **Switch friends list**) or use a **Dodo code**. If you decide to use a **Dodo code**, limit this to friends rather than the "more the merrier" option—it's always better to play online with people you know IRL. You can have a maximum of eight players (including yourself) on an island at one time, so you can have a lot of fun, but it's a good idea to set some rules. Anyone who visits your island can shake trees and collect what they drop and use your shop. While it's fine for people to sell their items in your store, you might want to ask them not to buy any of the limited items in **Nook's Cranny**. If you have a friend you really trust, you can add them to your **Best Friends list**. But watch out, **Best Friends** can use destructive tools like axes and shovels, which means they could damage something.

Return your seat to the upright position, and make sure your seat belt is securely fastened.

You can also visit other islands in your dreams. You just need the **Dream Address** code of where you want to go. It's a great way to get inspiration for how to make changes to your island.

Dos and Don'ts

DO ... ask a grown-up if you're allowed to visit someone's island (they may need to adjust parental controls for the session).

DON'T ... take anything from a friend's island without checking that it's OK first.

DO ... use reactions as a quick and fun way of communicating.

DON'T ... damage your friend's island—walk, don't run, otherwise you might trample their flowers by accident!

DO ... send a gift after you return home to say thank you (see page 46).

Game Ideas

Reaction Mirror: A great way of using the **reactions** function is to play a game a little like Simon Says. One player chooses a **reaction** at random, and the others have to copy it ... if they can! There are 44 reactions to unlock, but it will take awhile before you can collect them all.

Bug Net Tag: One of the funniest things to do in Animal Crossing is to swipe your bug net onto another character's head (you'll probably do it by accident at first when trying to catch a butterfly). If you have a group of friends all on the same island, one person can be "it" and hold a net. They have to chase the others around trying to net them. If you catch someone, they are now "it" and they'll need to get their net out.

Sending Messages

Everyone loves to receive letters and packages, right? It's no different in Animal Crossing. Here's how you do it ...

Whenever you log onto your game, it's always a treat to see the envelope flashing on your mailbox. What could it be? A present from Mom, your latest **Happy Home Academy rating**, a letter or gift from a fellow villager, something from a friend on another island, or maybe you forgot that you ordered something from **Nook Shopping** the day before? Whatever you find is always lovely to discover, so it's a good idea to find ways of sending things to others, too!

Message Board

If you're low on **Bells** or want to send a message to everyone on your island, you could just put a notice up on the message board by **Resident Services**. It's always a good idea to check the board each week anyway, so that you know about any upcoming fishing tourneys, but it's even better if you find a note from a friend who has visited your island.

July 19th, 2020

★ Upcoming Bug-Off ★
There's a Bug-Off coming up on Saturday, July 25th. I hear you can get prizes for catching lots of bugs. Don't miss out!

Isabelle

Going Postal

If you want to take the more personalized route, then head on down to **Dodo Airlines**. Just to the right of Orville, you will find a card stand. Pay **200 Bells** to send a letter or package to anyone on your island. You can also send messages to friends on other islands after you've first visited them, but you will need an **active internet connection** to do so.

Yellow wrapping paper

♪600   ♪160   ♪160   ♪480

♪2.680   ♪6.980   ♪280   ♪280

Timmy

**Oh! Changed your mind?
Anything else catch your eye?**

You can buy wrapping paper from **Nook's Cranny** to give your gifts something extra—animal villagers always love a wrapped gift!

Game Idea

Why not use the message board or send letters to other players to send them on a treasure hunt? You could wrap a gift and bury it somewhere on your island, then send someone a cryptic clue like this ...

Cross a bridge, and turn left after the second tree stump. Now follow the arrows until you find an "X marks the spot."

You can use a **Custom Design** of some arrows and display it on the ground.

Visitors to Your Island

There are many different creatures who you will find on your island from time to time. Let's take a closer look at some of them ...

It's impossible to predict when you will be visited by many of the animals in the game, since they don't work to a strict timetable. Redd (see page 28), for one, thrives on unpredictability. You're almost certain to have a traveling salescreature or a random visitor each day, so it's always worth checking the village square when you first play each day to see if there's an animal there. If not, check the beaches and other parts of the island ... or you might have to wait until night falls. It's always worth interacting with visiting animals, since there's almost always a reward of some kind.

There's also a pirate version of the shipwrecked seagull named Gullivarrr! He will reward you with a special pirate item.

Gulliver's Travels

From time to time, you will stumble across a shipwrecked seagull named Gulliver who has washed up on one of your beaches. You may have tried talking to him. Don't give up—you will need to talk to him LOTS before he stands up. He'll then ask you to find the missing parts of his communicator. As a reward, he will send you a souvenir from somewhere around the world the next day.

Ahoy there, Blossom!

Thanks to your help, I'm back with my crew! They made a big show of sighing and rolling their eyes when I climbed aboard. What jokers! Anyhoo, here's a cool trinket from my travels. Hope you enjoy it!

From Gulliver the Sailor

Island Life

Music Maestro

After your island reaches three-star status, K.K. Slider will start to hold weekly concerts outside **Resident Services**. These are a great way for the villagers to come together and have fun, but an added bonus is that you will be able to add to your music collection by speaking to him after 6 p.m. In the evening, he will take requests, and if you request something you don't yet have in your music collection (if you haven't been buying tracks yet, watch for them in **Nook Shopping**), he will give you a copy so you can listen to it any day of the week.

You can play K.K. Slider's music on your own music system (any stereo you own) by opening your music library on it and registering each track.

There are almost 100 K.K. Slider tracks to collect!

Ghostbuster

Wisp

TA-DA!

Have you ever thought you might be seeing ghosts on your island? At night, you can sometimes see a strange floating creature, but don't be scared. Wisp is much more scared of you than you should be of him! If you speak to him, he is so scared that five pieces of his spirit fly off to different parts of the island. If you catch them all with your net and return them to him, you'll be given the choice of two rewards.

Starry, Starry Night

Did you know that Blathers has a sister? Celeste wanders across your island on nights when meteor showers or shooting stars are due. She loves stargazing and is anxious to share DIY recipes that use star fragments. These fragments appear on the beaches the morning after you've wished upon a star. The best way to wish upon as many as possible is to head to the north of your island and angle your camera, so that you can see more of the sky. Make sure you're not holding any tools, then press A as soon as you see a star shooting across the sky. The more stars you wish upon, the more fragments you will find the next day.

One of the best recipes Celeste can give you is for a wand. This is a tool that allows you to charge it with up to eight outfits. It means you can change your clothes with just a wave of your wand!

Love Bug!

During the summer, a red lizard named Flick will challenge you once a month to catch as many bugs as you can within three minutes. You will be awarded points that you can exchange for a reward when you hit ten points. And it's always worth selling bugs to Flick rather than to **Nook's Cranny**—you're guaranteed to get more bucks for your bugs with him!

If you get enough points in the **Bug-Off** or **Fishing Tourney**, you can win a trophy!

Flick

Dedicate yourself to catching 3 of your chosen bug. When they have deemed you worthy, see me again.

Flick

A whole swarm!? This is the best day EVER! OK, tone it down Flick ...

Fishing Tourney

Four times a year, a beaver named C.J. will rock up to your island and hold a fishing tournament. You'll win points for the number of fish you catch in a set time. You can then cash in your points for a reward when you've earned at least ten. C.J. also turns up at other times and will set you a challenge.

Island Life

Always sell fish to C.J. when you get a chance. He will pay more for them than you can get at **Nook's Cranny**.

In exchange for three fish of the same kind, C.J. will make you a custom model of that fish to decorate your home with. Store them in your house until he turns up, since it can be hard to catch three rarer fish in one day.

Make sure you're carrying more than one rod—you don't want to be left without one if yours breaks!

Dig up some manila clams, and craft some bait, so that you don't have to run along the beach looking for a fishy shadow.

Now you're living in style, it's time to make the island your own ...

Customization's What You Need!

Learning DIY recipes and making items is just the beginning—there's so much more to crafting than first meets the eye.

After you've been playing the game for awhile, Tom Nook will offer you a **Customization Workshop** and present you with **50 kits** as a starter. You can buy more from Timmy and Tommy, so don't worry too much about using these up. **Customization Kits** and the ability to craft furniture from the same set will help you set up your **Happy Home Academy rating**, as well as make your house look super coordinated.

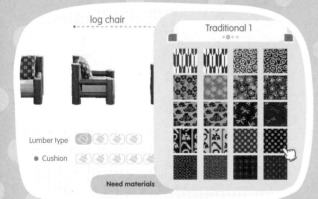

Take a look at the rooms in your fellow villagers' houses for inspiration— they tend to use furniture from a themed set to furnish their homes.

Making Friends

One of the trickiest animals to befriend is Sable. She sits at the back of **Able Sisters**, working hard at her sewing machine. Make sure you speak to her every day, and eventually, she will become less prickly. Not only will she tell you about her life, she will also give you new fabric patterns so you can customize your furniture.

Customizing an Area

You will probably come up with all kinds of cool ideas for different zones on your island. **Customization Kits** could be just what you need to give an area a unified look. Here is an idea for a small marketplace.

Step 1

Build four stands.

Step 2

Customize the stands using the same color wood and curtain pattern for each.

Step 3

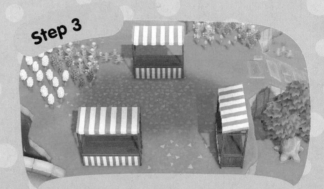

Clear an area of weeds and flowers, then place the stands.

Step 4

Create a path that will take players through the market. And add extra tables where you can.

Step 5

Add items that go together with the stands. Here, you can see a coffee stand, a plant stand, a fruit stand and a pottery stand.

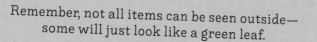

Remember, not all items can be seen outside—some will just look like a green leaf.

Island Fashion

The Able Sisters will keep you well-dressed for most occasions, but you might be missing an essential item, so what should you do? Make it yourself, of course!

The best way to start designing clothes is to go for the simpler option of **Custom Designs**—you're working with a flat design that can be applied to all kinds of things. Work up a design, and then you can wear it as a T-shirt or face paint. All you have to do is think about the design, and the game makes it work as an item of clothing. It gets more interesting, however, once you can access **Custom Designs Pro**—you can design T-shirts, hoodies, sweaters, dresses, and hats. You will also need to think carefully about the position of any pattern and how your clothing will look as a whole outfit.

Custom Designs isn't just for designing clothes—you can create artwork to hang on your wall or even a new path design (see page 60).

Go Pro!

Custom Designs Pro gives you so much more flexibility. Pick a clothing pattern—it's a little bit like a template that you "paint" your design onto—and then get started. You will work on each part of the item separately. The front, back, and sleeves of a T-shirt, for example, are all dealt with as distinct pieces that get "sewn" together by the game. There are guides that help you see where the center of the item is, to help you position a logo or make sure that two sides are symmetrical (or not, if you get experimental). The great thing is, you can see how your flat design transfers onto a 3D item of clothing when you look at the preview on the left—you can even spin it around using the right-hand joystick.

Island Designer

Sharing Your Designs

Other players can use your designs if you share them, using the **Custom Designs Kiosk** at the back of the **Able Sisters** shop. You can also find other players' designs here and transfer them to your **Custom Designs** interface (be careful, though—you only have a limited number of slots). You will need a **Nintendo Online subscription** to access the **Custom Designs Kiosk**.

You can display your designs along the back wall of the **Able Sisters** shop. Some of the villagers might even start wearing items you've designed!

55

Graphic Hoodie

The **Custom Designs Pro** interface can take a little getting used to, so this is a great place to start. Go for something simple and bold like this.

Making the cuffs and waist a contrasting color gives your design a more professional finish.

Happy T-shirt

What's not to love about this bright top? The trick is making sure that the design is centered—use the guides to help you.

Knitted Dress

It's all in the detail with this cute dress. You'll need to focus on getting the colors in the right squares for the trim of triangles and zigzags along the bottom and the sleeves.

Princess Dress

When you're feeling more confident, why not tackle a big, beautiful dress like this. Use different colors to create an optical illusion that the dress has many layers. You can do something similar to make it look like one item is a shirt, jacket, and tie.

You might want to change your hairstyle when wearing this design, so that it doesn't look too modern.

Island Designer

Experiment with edging designs. Remember to check the preview panel as squares on the flat design often look very different on the finished piece.

Cake Hat

Why not try something completely different? Hats that look like cakes are a popular challenge. The brim of the hat is the plate, and you can have a lot of fun decorating the cake.

Remember to add texture to make your cake look as real as possible.

Take Your Island to the Next Level

Whether you're struggling to reach the upper levels of your island or simply get over rivers, Tom Nook has the answer—although, as always, it will cost you!

You could simply continue using your vaulting pole and ladder to get to those hard-to-reach parts of your island, but careful use of bridges and inclines can really help you make your island experience even better. When Tom Nook suggests the possibility of adding infrastructure like this, it's a good idea to take him up on his offer. It might delay you in paying off your latest house debt, but improvements to your island will help you increase your star rating, so it's well worth it. Plus, all the other players on your Switch can help pay off the bridges or inclines, so it doesn't all fall to you.

Tom Nook

I want to expand.
I want to relocate.
Not now.

Time to talk about your home, hm? What shall we discuss?

Chat to Tom Nook about the ways you can change your island.

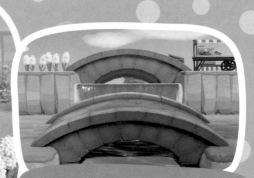

It can look good if you have two bridges of the same style near each other to create a scenic feature.

A Bridge Too Far?

There are eight bridge designs to choose from. They range from the cheap and simple log bridge, to the pricier zen bridge, red zen bridge, and iron bridge. It's up to you whether it's worth it to go for the expensive option! You might want to stick with one design across the entire island, or you could go for one of each style.

Sometimes you might need to dig up a tree or even move a building to get the position of a bridge just right.

You can have a maximum of eight bridges and eight inclines on your island. If you change your mind about the style or location of one, you can demolish it and start again.

Higher Ground

Again, there are eight designs to pick from. Natural ramps don't cost as many **Bells**, but you might want to go for steps rather than a slope. It's also worth considering which incline styles look best with each bridge style, to give your island a well-thought-out aesthetic.

Island Improvements

There are many ways that you can change your island's basic design. Here's where to get started ...

After your island has achieved a three-star rating (and K.K. Slider has performed his first concert), Tom Nook will send you a new app called **Island Designer**, which will allow you to reshape your island. At first, all you'll be able to do is lay a dirt path, but other path designs are available to you for **Nook Miles** when you visit the **Nook Stop**. You will also be able to buy permits for cliff construction and waterscaping, which gives you the

ability to create mountains and waterfalls, lakes and new rivers. It will probably take a little practice to "sculpt" your island the way you want it, but the results can be really impressive. With all this construction capability, you might realize that the buildings on your island aren't quite where you want them. Don't worry: Talk to Tom Nook, and he'll explain what to do.

Now I can make brick paths with my Island Designer app!

You might want to group all of your houses in one residential area, or have the stores next to each other.

Island Designer

Path to Success

There are seven path design permits you can buy, but the most interesting is probably the custom design path permit. This allows you to use your custom designs as a footpath. You could coordinate your paths with your clothes!

Get Lost!

You could use the ability to build cliffs to create a huge labyrinth for friends to try out when they visit your island. Bury a prize in the middle for the player who gets there first!

Island Inspiration

Not sure what to do with the rest of your island? This is just the place for you!

The only thing holding your island back is your inspiration … and DIY recipes … and what is available to buy in **Nook's Cranny** … and what might drop from the sky or tree … OK, so it will take quite a lot of work, but as you gather together the right recipes and items, you can build amazing outdoor themed areas for every animal to enjoy.

Monster Surprise

Hide one of these sculptures in the trees to give visitors a shock!

Outdoor Classroom

Every day's a school day when you build an outdoor learning space.

Teddy Bear Tea Party

As your teddy bear collection expands, you might want to have a picnic for them.

Viewpoint

Pick up a tourist telescope from **Nook Stop**, so visitors can admire the view of your island.

Island Designer

Playground

When you have enough **Nook Miles**, you can buy everything you need for a neat little playground.

Reading Room

Create a tranquil library so you can sit with a book ... or even write your own!

Boxing Ring

The boxing ring comes in four parts, so it will take awhile to get everything you need.

Your Island Checklist

Here are some targets that you need to aim for when playing Animal Crossing ...

Check off each action as you go!

- [ ] Convert your **tent** to a **house**.

- [ ] Get **K.K. Slider** to visit your island by achieving **three-star status**.

- [ ] Use **Custom Designs Pro** to create your own clothes, and display them in **Able Sisters**.

- [ ] One of the animals on your island **wears** one of your designs.

- [ ] Take photos of all the animals on your island at **Harvey's studio**.

- [ ] Collect all of **Sable**'s patterns (and use them).

- [ ] Landscape your island using **Island Designer** to create waterfalls and cliffs.

- [ ] Use **paths** to join up the different buildings on your island.

- [ ] Collect all of **Pascal**'s clothes and recipes.

- [ ] Collect all the fossils that **Blathers** needs.

- [ ] Complete your **Critterpedia** by collecting all the insects, fish, and sea creatures.

- [ ] Gain **golden tools**.

- [ ] Get an **upper floor**.

- [ ] Build a **basement**.

- [ ] Pay off all your **debt**.

- [ ] Achieve **five-star status**!